50 Delicious Premium Banana Dishes

By: Kelly Johnson

Table of Contents

- Bananas Foster
- Banana Bread
- Chocolate-Dipped Frozen Bananas
- Banana Cream Pie
- Caramelized Banana Pancakes
- Banana Pudding
- Banana Split
- Banana Muffins
- Banana Fritters
- Banana French Toast
- Banana Chia Pudding
- Banana Smoothie Bowl
- Banana Oatmeal Cookies
- Banana Upside-Down Cake
- Banana Walnut Cake
- Peanut Butter Banana Toast
- Banana Chocolate Chip Ice Cream
- Grilled Bananas with Honey
- Banana Coconut Rice Pudding
- Banana Beignets
- Deep-Fried Banana Rolls
- Banana Peanut Butter Milkshake
- Banana Cheesecake
- Banana Pancake Stack with Maple Syrup
- Banana Caramel Tart
- Banana Almond Granola Bars
- Banana Cinnamon Rolls
- Banana Chocolate Lava Cake
- Banana Soufflé
- Banana Yogurt Parfait
- Banana Mango Sorbet
- Banana and Nutella Crepes
- Roasted Bananas with Brown Sugar
- Banana Butter
- Banana Empanadas

- Banana and Avocado Mousse
- Banana Pecan Pie
- Banana and Honey Glazed Chicken
- Banana BBQ Glaze for Ribs
- Banana and Bacon Pancakes
- Spiced Banana Jam
- Banana and Ricotta Bruschetta
- Banana Curd Tart
- Banana and Cardamom Rice Kheer
- Banana and Passionfruit Ice Cream
- Banana and Dark Chocolate Brownies
- Banana Cornbread
- Banana and Rum Cake
- Banana Glazed Donuts
- Banana Marshmallow Fluff

Bananas Foster

Ingredients:

- 4 ripe bananas (cut lengthwise)
- 4 tbsp unsalted butter
- ½ cup brown sugar
- 1 tsp ground cinnamon
- ¼ cup dark rum
- (Optional) ¼ cup banana liqueur
- Vanilla ice cream (for serving)

Instructions:

1. In a large skillet over medium heat, melt the butter.
2. Stir in the brown sugar and cinnamon until the mixture becomes a syrup.
3. Add the banana halves and cook for 2–3 minutes until slightly softened.
4. Carefully pour in the rum (and banana liqueur, if using). If you're comfortable, ignite the alcohol to flambé; otherwise, let it simmer for a minute to evaporate the alcohol.
5. Once the flames subside (or after simmering), remove the pan from heat.
6. Spoon the bananas and syrup over scoops of vanilla ice cream and serve immediately.

Banana Bread

Ingredients:

- 2–3 very ripe bananas, mashed
- 1/3 cup melted unsalted butter
- ¾ cup sugar (adjust to taste)
- 1 large egg, beaten
- 1 tsp vanilla extract
- 1 tsp baking soda
- A pinch of salt
- 1½ cups all-purpose flour

Instructions:

1. Preheat your oven to 350°F (175°C) and grease a 9×5-inch loaf pan.
2. In a large bowl, mix the mashed bananas with the melted butter.
3. Stir in the sugar, egg, and vanilla extract.
4. Sprinkle in the baking soda and salt, then fold in the flour until just combined.
5. Pour the batter into the loaf pan and bake for 60–65 minutes or until a toothpick inserted in the center comes out clean.
6. Allow the bread to cool in the pan for a few minutes before transferring to a wire rack.

Chocolate-Dipped Frozen Bananas

Ingredients:

- 4 bananas (peeled and halved)
- 1 cup chocolate chips (dark or milk chocolate)
- 1 tbsp coconut oil
- Optional toppings: chopped nuts, sprinkles, shredded coconut

Instructions:

1. Insert a popsicle stick into each banana half and freeze them for at least 2 hours.
2. In a microwave-safe bowl, combine the chocolate chips and coconut oil. Microwave in 30-second bursts, stirring between intervals until smooth.
3. Dip each frozen banana into the melted chocolate, ensuring an even coat. Optionally, roll or sprinkle with your chosen toppings.
4. Return the bananas to the freezer for about 30 minutes until the chocolate sets, then serve.

Banana Cream Pie

Ingredients:

- 1 pre-baked pie crust (graham cracker or pastry)
- 3 ripe bananas (sliced)
- 2 cups whole milk
- ½ cup sugar
- ¼ cup all-purpose flour
- 3 egg yolks
- 2 tbsp unsalted butter
- 1 tsp vanilla extract
- Whipped cream (for topping)

Instructions:

1. In a saucepan, whisk together the sugar, flour, and egg yolks.
2. Gradually add the milk while stirring, and cook over medium heat until the mixture thickens into a custard.
3. Remove from heat and stir in the butter and vanilla extract.
4. Arrange the banana slices in the pre-baked crust, then pour the warm custard over the bananas.
5. Chill in the refrigerator for at least 4 hours until set.
6. Top with whipped cream before serving.

Caramelized Banana Pancakes

Ingredients:

- 2 ripe bananas (sliced)
- 1 cup pancake mix (or your favorite homemade pancake batter)
- ¾ cup milk (adjust as needed)
- 1 egg
- 2 tbsp melted butter (plus extra for the skillet)
- 1 tsp vanilla extract
- 2 tbsp brown sugar

Instructions:

1. Prepare your pancake batter by combining the pancake mix, milk, egg, melted butter, and vanilla extract.
2. In a separate skillet over medium heat, melt 2 tbsp butter and stir in the brown sugar until it dissolves into a syrup.
3. Add the banana slices to the skillet and cook until they caramelize (about 2 minutes per side). Remove and set aside.
4. Pour a ladleful of pancake batter into a buttered skillet and cook until bubbles form on the surface, then flip and cook until golden.
5. Serve the pancakes topped with the caramelized bananas and a drizzle of syrup if desired.

Banana Pudding

Ingredients:

- 4 ripe bananas (sliced)
- ½ cup sugar
- ¼ cup all-purpose flour
- 2 cups milk
- 3 egg yolks
- 1 tsp vanilla extract
- 1 box vanilla wafers
- (Optional) Whipped cream for topping

Instructions:

1. In a saucepan, whisk together the sugar, flour, and egg yolks.
2. Slowly whisk in the milk and cook over medium heat, stirring constantly until the mixture thickens into a custard.
3. Remove from heat and stir in the vanilla extract.
4. In a serving dish, layer vanilla wafers, banana slices, and custard. Repeat the layers.
5. Chill in the refrigerator for at least 2 hours before serving.
6. Top with whipped cream if desired.

Banana Split

Ingredients:

- 1 banana, split lengthwise
- 3 scoops of ice cream (typically vanilla, chocolate, and strawberry)
- Chocolate syrup
- Strawberry syrup
- Pineapple topping or sauce
- Whipped cream
- Chopped nuts
- 1 maraschino cherry (for garnish)

Instructions:

1. Place the split banana in a serving dish.
2. Arrange the three ice cream scoops between the banana halves.
3. Drizzle generously with chocolate, strawberry, and pineapple sauces.
4. Top with a swirl of whipped cream, a sprinkle of chopped nuts, and garnish with a maraschino cherry.
5. Serve immediately for a classic treat.

Banana Muffins

Ingredients:

- 1½ cups all-purpose flour
- 1 tsp baking powder
- ½ tsp baking soda
- ¼ tsp salt
- 3 ripe bananas, mashed
- ¾ cup sugar
- 1 large egg, lightly beaten
- ⅓ cup melted unsalted butter
- 1 tsp vanilla extract

Instructions:

1. Preheat your oven to 350°F (175°C). Grease a muffin tin or line with paper liners.
2. In one bowl, whisk together the flour, baking powder, baking soda, and salt.
3. In another bowl, mix the mashed bananas, sugar, egg, melted butter, and vanilla extract.
4. Combine the wet ingredients with the dry ingredients, stirring until just combined.
5. Divide the batter evenly among the muffin cups, filling each about 2/3 full.
6. Bake for 20–25 minutes or until a toothpick inserted in the center comes out clean.
7. Cool in the tin for 5 minutes before transferring to a wire rack.

Banana Fritters

Ingredients:

- 3 ripe bananas, cut into ½-inch thick rounds
- ½ cup all-purpose flour
- 2 tbsp sugar
- ¼ tsp salt
- ½ tsp baking powder
- ½ cup milk
- 1 large egg
- Oil for deep frying
- Powdered sugar (for dusting)

Instructions:

1. In a bowl, whisk together the flour, sugar, salt, and baking powder.
2. In another bowl, beat the milk and egg together, then add to the dry ingredients to form a smooth batter.
3. Heat oil in a deep skillet or fryer to 350°F (175°C).
4. Dip each banana slice into the batter, allowing excess to drip off.
5. Fry the battered banana rounds in batches until golden and crisp (about 2–3 minutes per side).
6. Drain on paper towels and dust lightly with powdered sugar before serving.

Banana French Toast

Ingredients:

- 4 slices of bread (preferably thick-cut)
- 2 ripe bananas, mashed
- 2 large eggs
- ½ cup milk
- 1 tsp vanilla extract
- ½ tsp ground cinnamon
- Butter for frying
- Maple syrup (for serving)

Instructions:

1. In a shallow bowl, whisk together the eggs, milk, mashed bananas, vanilla extract, and cinnamon.
2. Dip each bread slice into the mixture, ensuring both sides are well coated.
3. Heat butter in a skillet over medium heat.
4. Cook each slice for 2–3 minutes per side or until golden brown.
5. Serve hot with a drizzle of maple syrup.

Banana Chia Pudding

Ingredients:

- 2 ripe bananas, mashed
- ½ cup chia seeds
- 2 cups almond milk (or your preferred milk)
- 1–2 tbsp honey or maple syrup
- ½ tsp vanilla extract

Instructions:

1. In a bowl, mix the mashed bananas with almond milk, honey (or maple syrup), and vanilla extract.
2. Stir in the chia seeds until evenly distributed.
3. Cover and refrigerate for at least 4 hours or overnight, stirring once or twice during the first hour.
4. Stir again before serving. Garnish with extra banana slices, nuts, or a sprinkle of cinnamon if desired.

Banana Smoothie Bowl

Ingredients:

- 2 frozen bananas (sliced)
- ½ cup frozen berries (optional)
- ½ cup almond milk (or milk of choice)
- 1 tbsp honey or maple syrup
- Toppings: sliced banana, granola, chia seeds, coconut flakes, fresh berries

Instructions:

1. In a blender, combine the frozen bananas, berries, almond milk, and honey. Blend until smooth and thick.
2. Pour the smoothie into a bowl.
3. Top with your favorite toppings such as sliced banana, granola, chia seeds, coconut flakes, and fresh berries.
4. Enjoy immediately with a spoon.

Banana Oatmeal Cookies

Ingredients:

- 2 ripe bananas, mashed
- 1 ½ cups rolled oats
- ½ cup peanut butter
- ¼ cup honey or maple syrup
- ½ tsp vanilla extract
- ½ tsp cinnamon
- ¼ cup chocolate chips (optional)
- ¼ cup chopped walnuts (optional)

Instructions:

1. Preheat oven to 350°F (175°C) and line a baking sheet with parchment paper.
2. In a bowl, mix the mashed bananas, oats, peanut butter, honey, vanilla extract, and cinnamon.
3. Fold in the chocolate chips and walnuts if using.
4. Scoop tablespoon-sized portions onto the baking sheet and flatten slightly.
5. Bake for 12–15 minutes until lightly golden.
6. Let cool before serving.

Banana Upside-Down Cake

Ingredients:

- 2 ripe bananas, sliced
- ½ cup brown sugar
- 4 tbsp butter, melted
- 1 ½ cups all-purpose flour
- 1 tsp baking powder
- ½ tsp baking soda
- ½ tsp cinnamon
- ½ cup sugar
- 1 egg
- 1 tsp vanilla extract
- ½ cup milk

Instructions:

1. Preheat oven to 350°F (175°C). Grease a round cake pan.
2. Pour melted butter and brown sugar into the pan, spreading evenly.
3. Arrange banana slices on top in a single layer.
4. In a bowl, mix flour, baking powder, baking soda, and cinnamon.
5. In another bowl, beat sugar, egg, vanilla, and milk. Gradually mix in dry ingredients.
6. Pour the batter over the banana layer and bake for 30–35 minutes.
7. Let cool for 5 minutes before inverting onto a plate.

Banana Walnut Cake

Ingredients:

- 2 cups all-purpose flour
- 1 tsp baking soda
- ½ tsp salt
- 1 tsp cinnamon
- ½ cup butter, softened
- ¾ cup sugar
- 2 eggs
- 1 tsp vanilla extract
- 3 ripe bananas, mashed
- ½ cup buttermilk
- ¾ cup chopped walnuts

Instructions:

1. Preheat oven to 350°F (175°C). Grease a cake pan.
2. Whisk flour, baking soda, salt, and cinnamon in a bowl.
3. In another bowl, beat butter and sugar, then add eggs and vanilla.
4. Mix in mashed bananas and buttermilk. Gradually fold in dry ingredients and walnuts.
5. Pour into the cake pan and bake for 35–40 minutes.

Peanut Butter Banana Toast

Ingredients:

- 2 slices of whole-grain bread
- 2 tbsp peanut butter
- 1 banana, sliced
- 1 tsp honey
- A pinch of cinnamon

Instructions:

1. Toast the bread slices.
2. Spread peanut butter evenly over each slice.
3. Top with banana slices, drizzle with honey, and sprinkle with cinnamon.

Banana Chocolate Chip Ice Cream

Ingredients:

- 3 ripe bananas, frozen and sliced
- ¼ cup milk (or dairy-free alternative)
- ¼ cup chocolate chips
- 1 tsp vanilla extract

Instructions:

1. Blend frozen bananas, milk, and vanilla extract until smooth.
2. Stir in chocolate chips.
3. Freeze for 30 minutes for a firmer texture or serve immediately as soft serve.

Grilled Bananas with Honey

Ingredients:

- 2 ripe bananas, peeled and halved lengthwise
- 2 tbsp honey
- 1 tbsp butter, melted
- ½ tsp cinnamon

Instructions:

1. Preheat grill or grill pan to medium heat.
2. Brush bananas with melted butter and place on the grill.
3. Cook for 2–3 minutes per side until grill marks appear.
4. Drizzle with honey and sprinkle with cinnamon before serving.

Banana Coconut Rice Pudding

Ingredients:

- 1 cup cooked jasmine rice
- 1 cup coconut milk
- ½ cup milk
- ¼ cup sugar
- 1 ripe banana, mashed
- 1 tsp vanilla extract
- ½ tsp cinnamon

Instructions:

1. In a saucepan, combine coconut milk, milk, sugar, and mashed banana.
2. Add the cooked rice and simmer for 10–15 minutes until thick.
3. Stir in vanilla and cinnamon, then serve warm or chilled.

Banana Beignets

Ingredients:

- 2 ripe bananas, mashed
- 1 ¼ cups all-purpose flour
- ½ tsp baking powder
- ¼ tsp salt
- 2 tbsp sugar
- ½ tsp cinnamon
- ½ cup milk
- 1 egg
- Oil for frying
- Powdered sugar for dusting

Instructions:

1. Heat oil to 350°F (175°C).
2. In a bowl, whisk flour, baking powder, salt, sugar, and cinnamon.
3. Stir in mashed bananas, milk, and egg until smooth.
4. Drop spoonfuls of batter into the hot oil and fry until golden brown.
5. Drain on paper towels and dust with powdered sugar.

Deep-Fried Banana Rolls

Ingredients:

- 4 ripe bananas
- 4 egg roll wrappers
- 2 tbsp brown sugar
- 1 tsp cinnamon
- Oil for frying

Instructions:

1. Peel bananas and cut in half.
2. Mix brown sugar and cinnamon and sprinkle over bananas.
3. Wrap each banana piece in an egg roll wrapper and seal the edges with water.
4. Heat oil to 350°F (175°C) and fry until golden brown.

Banana Peanut Butter Milkshake

Ingredients:

- 2 ripe bananas
- 2 cups vanilla ice cream
- ½ cup milk
- ¼ cup peanut butter
- 1 tsp honey

Instructions:

1. Blend all ingredients until smooth.
2. Pour into a glass and enjoy immediately.

Banana Cheesecake

Ingredients:

Crust:

- 1 ½ cups graham cracker crumbs
- ¼ cup melted butter

Filling:

- 2 (8 oz) cream cheese blocks, softened
- ½ cup sugar
- 2 ripe bananas, mashed
- 2 eggs
- 1 tsp vanilla extract
- ½ cup sour cream

Instructions:

1. Preheat oven to 325°F (160°C). Mix crust ingredients and press into a springform pan.
2. Beat cream cheese and sugar until smooth. Add mashed bananas, eggs, vanilla, and sour cream.
3. Pour over the crust and bake for 50–55 minutes.
4. Chill before serving.

Banana Pancake Stack with Maple Syrup

Ingredients:

- 2 ripe bananas, mashed
- 1 cup all-purpose flour
- 1 tsp baking powder
- ½ tsp cinnamon
- 1 egg
- ¾ cup milk
- 1 tbsp butter, melted
- 1 tsp vanilla extract
- Maple syrup, for serving

Instructions:

1. In a bowl, mix flour, baking powder, and cinnamon.
2. In another bowl, whisk mashed bananas, egg, milk, butter, and vanilla.
3. Gradually add dry ingredients to the wet mixture, stirring until combined.
4. Heat a pan over medium heat and cook pancakes for 2–3 minutes per side.
5. Stack pancakes and drizzle with maple syrup before serving.

Banana Caramel Tart

Ingredients:

Crust:

- 1 ½ cups graham cracker crumbs
- ¼ cup melted butter

Filling:

- 3 ripe bananas, sliced
- 1 cup heavy cream
- ½ cup sugar
- 2 tbsp butter
- 1 tsp vanilla extract
- ½ tsp sea salt

Instructions:

1. Preheat oven to 350°F (175°C). Mix graham cracker crumbs with melted butter and press into a tart pan. Bake for 10 minutes, then cool.
2. In a saucepan, heat sugar over medium heat until melted and amber in color.
3. Stir in butter, then slowly add heavy cream while whisking. Add vanilla and salt.
4. Layer banana slices over the tart crust and pour caramel sauce on top.
5. Chill for at least 2 hours before serving.

Banana Almond Granola Bars

Ingredients:

- 2 ripe bananas, mashed
- 2 cups rolled oats
- ½ cup almond butter
- ¼ cup honey
- ½ cup chopped almonds
- ½ tsp cinnamon
- 1 tsp vanilla extract

Instructions:

1. Preheat oven to 325°F (160°C) and line a baking pan with parchment paper.
2. Mix all ingredients in a bowl until well combined.
3. Press mixture into the baking pan and bake for 20–25 minutes.
4. Let cool before cutting into bars.

Banana Cinnamon Rolls

Ingredients:

Dough:

- 2 ½ cups all-purpose flour
- 2 tbsp sugar
- 1 packet (2 ¼ tsp) yeast
- ½ cup warm milk
- 2 tbsp butter, melted
- 1 mashed banana
- 1 egg

Filling:

- ½ cup brown sugar
- 1 tbsp cinnamon
- 2 tbsp butter, softened
- 1 banana, thinly sliced

Instructions:

1. In a bowl, mix yeast, warm milk, and sugar. Let sit for 5 minutes.
2. Add flour, mashed banana, egg, and melted butter. Knead for 5 minutes, then let rise for 1 hour.
3. Roll out dough into a rectangle and spread butter over it.
4. Sprinkle brown sugar and cinnamon, then add banana slices.
5. Roll up and slice into 8 rolls. Place in a greased pan and let rise for 30 minutes.
6. Bake at 350°F (175°C) for 20–25 minutes.

Banana Chocolate Lava Cake

Ingredients:

- ½ cup dark chocolate, melted
- ¼ cup butter
- ½ cup sugar
- 2 eggs
- 1 mashed banana
- ¼ cup flour
- 1 tsp vanilla extract

Instructions:

1. Preheat oven to 375°F (190°C). Grease 4 ramekins.
2. In a bowl, mix melted chocolate and butter.
3. Stir in sugar, eggs, mashed banana, flour, and vanilla.
4. Pour batter into ramekins and bake for 10–12 minutes.
5. Serve warm with ice cream.

Banana Soufflé

Ingredients:

- 2 ripe bananas, mashed
- 3 egg whites
- ¼ cup sugar
- ½ tsp vanilla extract

Instructions:

1. Preheat oven to 375°F (190°C). Grease ramekins.
2. Beat egg whites with sugar until stiff peaks form.
3. Fold in mashed bananas and vanilla extract.
4. Pour into ramekins and bake for 12–15 minutes.

Banana Yogurt Parfait

Ingredients:

- 1 ripe banana, sliced
- 1 cup Greek yogurt
- ½ cup granola
- 1 tbsp honey

Instructions:

1. In a glass, layer yogurt, banana slices, granola, and honey.
2. Repeat layers and serve immediately.

Banana Mango Sorbet

Ingredients:

- 2 ripe bananas, frozen
- 1 ripe mango, chopped
- 1 tbsp honey
- Juice of 1 lime

Instructions:

1. Blend all ingredients until smooth.
2. Freeze for 1 hour before serving.

Banana and Nutella Crepes

Ingredients:

Crepes:

- 1 cup flour
- 1 cup milk
- 1 egg
- 1 tbsp sugar
- 1 tbsp melted butter

Filling:

- 2 bananas, sliced
- ½ cup Nutella

Instructions:

1. Whisk crepe ingredients until smooth.
2. Cook thin crepes in a buttered pan.
3. Spread Nutella and add banana slices. Fold and serve.

Roasted Bananas with Brown Sugar

Ingredients:

- 2 bananas, halved lengthwise
- 2 tbsp brown sugar
- 1 tbsp butter

Instructions:

1. Preheat oven to 375°F (190°C).
2. Place bananas on a baking sheet and sprinkle with brown sugar and butter.
3. Roast for 10–12 minutes.

Banana Butter

Ingredients:

- 2 ripe bananas, mashed
- ¼ cup butter, softened
- 2 tbsp honey
- ½ tsp cinnamon

Instructions:

1. Blend all ingredients until smooth.
2. Store in a jar and refrigerate.

Banana Empanadas

Ingredients:

Dough:

- 2 cups all-purpose flour
- ½ tsp salt
- ½ cup butter, cold and cubed
- ¼ cup water

Filling:

- 2 ripe bananas, mashed
- 2 tbsp brown sugar
- ½ tsp cinnamon

Instructions:

1. Mix flour and salt. Cut in butter, then add water to form a dough.
2. Roll out dough and cut into circles.
3. Mix filling ingredients and place a spoonful in each circle.
4. Fold, seal, and bake at 375°F (190°C) for 15–20 minutes.

Banana and Avocado Mousse

Ingredients:

- 1 ripe banana
- 1 ripe avocado
- 2 tbsp cocoa powder
- 1 tbsp honey
- 1 tsp vanilla extract

Instructions:

1. Blend all ingredients until smooth.
2. Chill for 30 minutes before serving.

Banana Pecan Pie

Ingredients:

Crust:

- 1 ½ cups all-purpose flour
- ½ cup butter, cold and cubed
- ¼ tsp salt
- ¼ cup ice water

Filling:

- 3 ripe bananas, mashed
- ¾ cup brown sugar
- ½ cup corn syrup
- 2 eggs
- 1 tsp vanilla extract
- 1 tsp cinnamon
- 1 ½ cups pecans

Instructions:

1. Preheat oven to 350°F (175°C).
2. For the crust, mix flour and salt, cut in butter, then add ice water to form a dough. Roll out and fit into a pie pan.
3. In a bowl, whisk eggs, brown sugar, corn syrup, vanilla, and cinnamon. Add mashed bananas and mix well.
4. Stir in pecans and pour into crust.
5. Bake for 45–50 minutes until set. Cool before serving.

Banana and Honey Glazed Chicken

Ingredients:

- 4 chicken thighs or breasts
- 1 ripe banana, mashed
- ¼ cup honey
- 2 tbsp soy sauce
- 1 tbsp Dijon mustard
- 2 cloves garlic, minced
- ½ tsp black pepper
- 1 tbsp olive oil

Instructions:

1. Preheat oven to 375°F (190°C).
2. Mix mashed banana, honey, soy sauce, mustard, garlic, and black pepper.
3. Coat chicken with the glaze and marinate for 30 minutes.
4. Heat olive oil in a pan and sear chicken for 3 minutes per side.
5. Transfer to a baking dish and bake for 20–25 minutes.

Banana BBQ Glaze for Ribs

Ingredients:

- 1 ripe banana, mashed
- ½ cup ketchup
- ¼ cup brown sugar
- 2 tbsp apple cider vinegar
- 1 tbsp Worcestershire sauce
- 1 tsp smoked paprika
- 1 tsp garlic powder
- ½ tsp cayenne pepper
- ½ tsp salt

Instructions:

1. In a saucepan, combine all ingredients and bring to a simmer. Cook for 5 minutes.
2. Brush over ribs during the last 10 minutes of grilling or roasting.

Banana and Bacon Pancakes

Ingredients:

- 1 ripe banana, mashed
- 1 cup all-purpose flour
- 1 tbsp sugar
- 1 tsp baking powder
- ½ tsp cinnamon
- 1 egg
- ¾ cup milk
- 2 tbsp butter, melted
- 4 strips bacon, cooked and crumbled

Instructions:

1. In a bowl, whisk flour, sugar, baking powder, and cinnamon.
2. In another bowl, mix banana, egg, milk, and melted butter.
3. Combine wet and dry ingredients, then fold in crumbled bacon.
4. Cook pancakes in a greased pan over medium heat until golden brown.

Spiced Banana Jam

Ingredients:

- 3 ripe bananas, mashed
- ½ cup sugar
- ½ tsp cinnamon
- ¼ tsp nutmeg
- 1 tbsp lemon juice
- ½ tsp vanilla extract

Instructions:

1. In a saucepan, combine bananas, sugar, cinnamon, nutmeg, and lemon juice.
2. Cook over medium heat, stirring, for 10–15 minutes.
3. Remove from heat and stir in vanilla.
4. Let cool and store in a jar.

Banana and Ricotta Bruschetta

Ingredients:

- 1 baguette, sliced
- 1 cup ricotta cheese
- 2 ripe bananas, sliced
- 2 tbsp honey
- 1 tbsp chopped walnuts

Instructions:

1. Toast baguette slices until golden.
2. Spread ricotta on each slice, then top with banana slices.
3. Drizzle with honey and sprinkle with walnuts.

Banana Curd Tart

Ingredients:

Crust:

- 1 ½ cups crushed graham crackers
- ¼ cup melted butter
- 2 tbsp sugar

Banana Curd:

- 3 ripe bananas, mashed
- ½ cup sugar
- 2 egg yolks
- 2 tbsp butter
- 1 tbsp lemon juice
- ½ tsp vanilla extract

Instructions:

1. Preheat oven to 350°F (175°C). Mix graham cracker crumbs with butter and sugar, press into a tart pan, and bake for 10 minutes. Cool.
2. In a saucepan, combine bananas, sugar, egg yolks, and lemon juice. Cook over low heat, stirring, until thickened.
3. Remove from heat, stir in butter and vanilla. Cool before pouring into the crust.
4. Chill for at least 2 hours before serving.

Banana and Cardamom Rice Kheer

Ingredients:

- ½ cup basmati rice
- 4 cups whole milk
- ¼ cup sugar
- ½ tsp cardamom powder
- 2 ripe bananas, mashed
- 2 tbsp chopped nuts (almonds/pistachios)
- 1 tbsp raisins

Instructions:

1. Rinse and soak rice for 30 minutes.
2. In a saucepan, bring milk to a boil. Add rice and simmer, stirring often, for 30 minutes.
3. Stir in sugar, cardamom, mashed banana, nuts, and raisins. Cook for 5 more minutes.
4. Serve warm or chilled.

Banana and Passionfruit Ice Cream

Ingredients:

- 3 ripe bananas, frozen
- ½ cup passionfruit pulp
- ¼ cup honey
- ½ cup coconut milk

Instructions:

1. Blend all ingredients until smooth.
2. Transfer to a container and freeze for 2–3 hours before serving.

Banana and Dark Chocolate Brownies

Ingredients:

- 2 ripe bananas, mashed
- ½ cup butter, melted
- ¾ cup sugar
- 2 eggs
- 1 tsp vanilla extract
- ½ cup cocoa powder
- ½ cup flour
- ½ tsp salt
- ½ cup dark chocolate chunks

Instructions:

1. Preheat oven to 350°F (175°C). Grease a baking pan.
2. Whisk melted butter, sugar, eggs, vanilla, and bananas.
3. Stir in cocoa, flour, and salt. Fold in chocolate chunks.
4. Pour into pan and bake for 25–30 minutes.

Banana Cornbread

Ingredients:

- 1 cup cornmeal
- 1 cup all-purpose flour
- 1 tbsp baking powder
- ½ tsp salt
- 1 ripe banana, mashed
- 1 cup buttermilk
- ¼ cup honey
- 1 egg
- ¼ cup melted butter

Instructions:

1. Preheat oven to 375°F (190°C). Grease a baking dish.
2. In a bowl, mix cornmeal, flour, baking powder, and salt.
3. In another bowl, whisk banana, buttermilk, honey, egg, and melted butter.
4. Combine wet and dry ingredients, pour into the dish, and bake for 25 minutes.

Banana and Rum Cake

Ingredients:

- 2 ripe bananas, mashed
- ½ cup butter, softened
- ¾ cup brown sugar
- 2 eggs
- 1 ½ cups flour
- 1 tsp baking soda
- ½ tsp cinnamon
- ¼ cup dark rum
- ½ cup chopped walnuts

Instructions:

1. Preheat oven to 350°F (175°C). Grease a cake pan.
2. Cream butter and sugar. Add eggs and mashed bananas.
3. Stir in flour, baking soda, cinnamon, and rum. Fold in walnuts.
4. Pour into the pan and bake for 40 minutes.

Banana Glazed Donuts

Ingredients:

Dough:

- 2 cups flour
- ½ cup sugar
- 1 tsp baking powder
- ½ tsp cinnamon
- 1 ripe banana, mashed
- ½ cup milk
- 1 egg
- 2 tbsp melted butter

Glaze:

- 1 banana, mashed
- 1 cup powdered sugar
- 1 tbsp milk

Instructions:

1. Preheat oven to 350°F (175°C). Grease a donut pan.
2. Mix dry ingredients. In another bowl, whisk banana, milk, egg, and butter. Combine both mixtures.
3. Pipe into the donut pan and bake for 15 minutes.
4. For the glaze, whisk banana, powdered sugar, and milk. Dip donuts in glaze.

Banana Marshmallow Fluff

Ingredients:

- 2 ripe bananas, mashed
- ½ cup sugar
- ¼ cup water
- 1 egg white
- ¼ tsp vanilla extract

Instructions:

1. In a saucepan, heat sugar and water to a boil until it reaches 240°F (115°C).
2. Beat egg white until soft peaks form.
3. Slowly pour the hot syrup into the egg white while beating.
4. Fold in mashed bananas and vanilla.

www.ingramcontent.com/pod-product-compliance
Lightning Source LLC
LaVergne TN
LVHW081335060526
838201LV00055B/2667